HOW I FEEL ABOUT JERMAL...

How I Feel About Jermal...

THE LOVE OF FAMILY & FRIENDS

Amy L. Deanes

Love Ones of Pastor Boddie

Superior Publishing LLC.

Contents

Dedication	ix
TO EVERYONE I'M SOMEONE...	1
FREE BODDIE	**3**
INTRODUCTION	5
1 How I Feel About Myself	8
2 IT SHIFTED...LIKE GOD SAID	12
3 HE CALLS ME TEE TEE	16
4 HE IS TOUGH ON US MINISTERS	17
5 THE DAY I MET AN ANGEL	19
6 YOU TOOK THE LITTLE GOD GAVE YOU	21
7 V.I.P. STATUS	23

8
WHAT GOES ON IN BILOXI STAYS IN BILOXI 25

9
HE WHIPPED ME LIKE HE WAS MY DADDY 27

10
HE SAW SOMETHING IN ME 29

11
HE PULLED SOMETHING OUT OF ME 31

12
HE KNOWS HOW TO REEL IT IN... 33

13
HE NEVER CLOSED THE DOORS DURING THE PANDEMIC 35

14
HE CALLS ME HIS HONORARY MEMBER 37

15
YOU NEVER JUDGED HIM 38

16
YOU DIDN'T HESISTATE 40

17
HE REACHES OUT TO ME FIRST 42

18
HE WILL LAUGH WHEN YOU LAUGH AND CRY WHEN YOU CRY 44

19
I KNEW THAT HE WAS DIFFERENT 46

20
HE TELLS IT LIKE IT IS 48

21
HE'S BEEN THROUGH A STORM LIKE US   50

22
I KNOW HOW HARD YOU'VE BEEN WORKING   51

23
A POEM FOR PASTOR BODDIE   52

24
WE ARE BLESSED TO HAVE YOU   55

25
EMARIE   57

26
MY DAD TAUGHT ME NOTHING IS IMPOSSIBLE   58

27
I LEARN FROM HIM...   59

28
MY DAD HAS DONE MANY THINGS FOR ME   60

29
IT'S SOMETHING ABOUT YOU THAT MAKES IT HARD TO SAY NO   61

30
BIG BROTHER, LITTLE BROTHER   63

31
YOU MADE SURE YOU SHARED WITH ME   67

32
YOU ARE PROBABLY WONDERING WHY EVERYONE CALLS HIM JERMAL   69

HE IS VERY SUPPORTIVE TO HIS FAMILY AND FRIENDS   73

33
CLASS OF 87   75

34
THERE IS NO WAY ONE MAD DID ALL OF THAT   77

35
HE PREACHED ON A LEVEL ALL GROUPS AND
AGES COULD UNDERSTAND   80

36
GREATER GRACE   83

37
HE JUST KEPT SAYING WATCH GOD   84

38
HE'S NOT A FRIEND OF MINE, BUT MY BIG
BROTHER   87

39
YOU HAVE ALWAYS BEEN A TRUE BROTHER   89

40
HIS YES IS A YES   92

41
FRIENDS TIL THE END   94

About The Author   96

Dedicated to the Memory of
Claud, Sr and Emma Jean Boddie
in honor of
Pastor Jermal Boddie, Sr's 5th Year
Church Anniversary at
Grace Baptist Church, Okolona, MS

Copyright © 2021 by Amy L. Deanes & The Family & Friends of Pastor Jermal Boddie, Sr

All rights reserved. No part of this book may be reproduced in any manner whatsoever without written permission except in the case of brief quotations embodied in critical articles and reviews.

Superior Publishing LLC., 2021

TO EVERYONE I'M SOMEONE...

Pastor Elliott Jermal Boddie, Sr.
Sisters, Brother and Friends donated pictures for this project

Signature:_____

Date: _____

FREE BODDIE

It was behind the prison wall
you heeded to the Master's call
You were not made to be contained
not even behind a 6X8 frame.
Maybe it kept you for a minute
to grab your attention
brought you through the 80 year sentence.
Even that didn't last long,
You couldn't be held, God's will was too strong
The world was waiting for Boddie to be free
the People in Egypt were in Misery.
Went in Boddie, came out parting the Red Sea
Moses with the Rod, no matter what you had done.
God had dealt with the heart, made you ready for EVERYONE
Even the haters too, they needed to see that God sent you
if nothing more but just to free me!
Before you got to me, you establish Grace AND the community.
Sonya says it all the time, she Thank God for this place!
This is a Refuge, God erected through you.
A place to pull off our shoes and let God do what HE do.
Everyone comes in and say, "What a sweet spirit in this place"
Through your crying, suffering and worship, seeking HIS face.
It's just what it cost to be in this space.

Amy L. Deanes

INTRODUCTION

WHO IS BODDIE?

So this guy named Jermal Boddie, Sr. was born to touch the lives of everyone he has touched and those yet to come. We all share this common bond, we know Pastor Boddie in our own way. And we can all say that he is just plain real. He is the same in and out of the pulpit. He carries himself in a way that is approachable. Even though in appearance sometimes he looks arrogant and blunt he is one of the most down to earth people you would ever meet. If he is for you, he is for you all the way! And so often he says, 'You either with me or against me!"

He has never met a stranger. He is wise and very observant. He watches and stays in tune with what's going on in the world, the community, the church and with his family. Who and what he loves, he loves hard.

I remember him saying in a setting, whether it was bible class or regular service, that he has an addictive spirit. Once he starts with something he becomes addicted to it. Oh yeah, that was a sermon, HE was addicted to JESUS. He was a JESUS JUNKIE! He talked about being hooked on a lot of things until he got a HIT of CHRIST and He's been Cracked OUT every since. He loves church, like more than anyone I know. My momma loves church, but Boddie LOOOVES church. In mid-conversation about a scripture, about Sunday service, about life, about whatever he'll say,

"Ay let everybody know, we gonna do a Pop-Up service tonight at 7pm. Only those that want it will come!" And I'm sitting there holding the phone like, "Huh tonight Pastor Boddie?"

"Yeah you can't hear now?" Oh his personality I had to learn because, Lord knows this man has a smart mouth. So then I'm like, "It's gonna be a short notice" and of course he always had a come back, "It's a sacrifice!"

I remember my first "fussing" encounter with him, he was going off about the church being cleaned up....Oh my goodness, he called me and went off. He called Tangi and went off and then I think he called Evangelist Linda and went off. He was like a tornado. "So I wasn't used to a Pastor fussing at me and saying whatever. But he means business about that church. When the dust settled he called and of course NOT to apologize but tell me why he was so upset.

"If you don't love it, nobody else will. God can't give you BIGGER if you won't take care of the little. Your house can be dirty or nasty, but not the Lord's house." I understood what he meant and because he loved it like that, made me love it. Because he loved having service all the time made us love it.

Pastor Boddie's flock loves him. They love him because he is them. He is one that visits, gives, meddles and jokes, he texts, he calls even if it's not a long conversation. He does whats best for the church. And he pumps up the men and women in the church....he notices everything and everybody. If you have a new hairdo, Lord he will announce it and then Deacon Walker gets on the band wagon with him. A new suit or new shoes, Pastor will make sure everyone notices it. If you are shy, you won't be after an encounter with PB. He is definitely one of a kind. I admire how he makes us all feel, loved. He is the one that God gave to shepherd over us. Even though, he is the Pastor he isn't so high, that he doesn't show emotion or pain. Even in his vulnerability we see his strength. I have never been in a church like this. But we've learned that it's okay to show emotion. It's okay to give God your all and your best! God deserves nothing but the best.

When the Lord laid it on my heart to do this I got excited because I know he deserves it. He has done so much for so many people like it's just second nature to jump in and help. I remember when I first came to Grace Baptist Church and I was at my mom's house and the Lord gave me a scripture for PB. So of course I went and read it first and sent it to him, it was **Revelation 3:8 NIV I know your deeds. See, I have placed before you an open door that no one can shut. I know that you have little strength, yet you have kept my word and have not denied my name.**

And I knew then, that I was where God wanted me to be for however long I was to be there. The Lord assured me through that scripture to him, that I was at the right place.

1

How I Feel About Myself

Minister Amy asked how did I feel about myself for this write up, (which he will find out later it wasn't for a newspaper) I really feel good about myself and the reason why is because God has granted me this opportunity to get it right. My past, when I was young, I was out of control just being honest. So now I'm making better decisions in my life.

The question was asked if I could change anything what would it be, If I could change anything it would be not having children everywhere. Because they deserve better than what I did but God is making everything up. We have beautiful relationships.

My greatest fun moments are all when I was young, when I stole catfish on the white man's pond. He saw us and start shooting I ran straight through a barbed wire fence. Then stealing peaches off the neighbor's tree, I heard a shot and I fell from the tree thought I had been shot. And another time which also involved stealing. When I was stealing plums off of Miss Avery's tree. She told me I couldn't have any plums, so I came back with a saw and I cut down the tree and drug it down the road.

What I love about being a Pastor? I love the fact of giving people an opportunity to get saved and just to give them hope! When God called me to preach, I felt special because why would he choose somebody like me?? I mean, my background was all jacked up, my name was mud in the community! So why would God choose somebody like me?

I owe God because HE SAVED my life!!!

He saved me from hell and from my OWNSELF!!! I was on my way to hell. I didn't love myself. I was mistreating my body with drugs, alcohol and sex. That's why I praise and worship God the way that I do. I can never repay Him but I can show my gratitude.

2

IT SHIFTED...LIKE GOD SAID

 After being rejected, I was losing hope. I began to question God, "Why did you call me and not give me an opportunity?" I felt at my lowest. It seemed to me like all eyes were on me, like, "What you gonna do now, you stepped out there saying God called you, and you have no where to preach?" That's how I felt. All the minsters were being acknowledged, except for me. Sunday after Sunday, I felt my heart sink lower and lower. I made up my mind not to go back to church. I was not going to continue to sit in humiliation. Other people were reaching out to me, "Come Here, Go over there!" But the Lord continued to tell me, "No!" I cried some more, ended up going back to church again. Even though I said, I wasn't going back, I couldn't stay away either. The intensity grew....I began to pray for my feelings to change. I didn't want to be bitter or hateful. I just wanted the hurt and disappointment to go away.

 I was driving and praying one night on my way from a photo-shoot, crying as usual upset about my circumstances. The Lord didn't answer me at the moment, but when I arrived home, got out of my shoes the

Lord spoke. He said, "I'm going to free you tonight" Those were His exact words, made my heart race and tears well up in my eyes again. I was just so emotional. I began to edit the pictures that I had taken and received a message on Messenger. I didn't look at it right away because I wanted to finish working before doing anything else. Messenger went off again, so I checked it and one of the messages was Jermal Boddie. In my mind, I was thinking, what could he want. I had met him a time before, he reached out to me through Facebook to come and pray at a Wednesday Night Worship Service. So after I opened the message it said, Woman of God give me a call at this number. I replied, "Okay Pastor when I get done working I will, my phone is my hotspot."

I gave Pastor Jermal Boddie, Sr a phone call, and being a trained 911 Operator the first thing I listen for on every phone call is the background noise. And it was noisy. He and his children were cooking something. He spoke very loudly, "Minister, the Lord told me to free you! I need you to come and be my Assistant Pastor!" I almost dropped the phone. I couldn't say a word. He said, "Hello are you there?" and I could only reply, "Free me how?" He had a smart mouth, He said, "Are you hard of hearing I said, Come be my Assistant Pastor." I said, I don't even get to preach at my own church!" He said, "I didn't ask you all that, I'm just saying what the Lord told me. Can you come and be my Assistant?" I said, "Well let me pray about that." I was about to pass out. He replied, "You already prayed about it, that's why the Lord had me to reach out to you, cause you been praying about it, but Go ahead I understand how yall do, yall pray about something and when the Lord give it to you, you want to pray some more!" He went on to say that he didn't believe in women preaching either that God had dealt with him and it wasn't long ago. And I replied, I didn't believe either until he called me to do it. So I got off the phone and called my mom, who of course was excited, but told me to pray about it. I prayed and almost unable to sleep that night. On my way to work the next morning the Lord answered me. The Lord said unto me, "If you go, your life will shift!" My life has been shifting every since in Jesus name lows and highs. My last Easter at my home church was The Easter of 2018.

Pastor Boddie just turned me a loose. He was like, "Preach on this day, I'll be out of town" I was like, "You won't be here?" He was like, "You a preacher, preach, I don't have to be there, say what the Lord tells you." He pushed me hard. Sometimes I felt he was pushing me too hard. I almost wanted to just leave. I felt he was too demanding....He wanted things to be perfect. He always said, "You do your best for God! I don't play about preaching, teaching, worshiping and praising God! We give our best!" I was late a lot and he called me in the office and told me, "Leaders are on time! You are a born leader, you don't lead from behind. Leaders lead out front. Be an example." I didn't like care a lot for correction, but I began to see he was helping me become my best for the Lord. He often told me that the Lord told him to train me how to do everything, get me ready to Pastor one day. He fussed at me about not singing, he told me, "Use every gift God gave you, that's why HE gave it to you to use it. Then he would send me songs, "Daughter Learn this, Daughter you did good on this, but get with Jerimane and work on this!"

He called one day, "Daughter it's time for you to be licensed!" Joy filled my heart. He said we will do it at Mt. Calvary it's bigger. Invite your home church. Invite all your friends and family, this is gonna be a big day for you!

Here it is again, September 19, 2021, My father in the Ministry ordained me. I can go on and on about Pastor Boddie. But I can say that he reached out to me and then looked out for me. Even though he fusses a lot....I know he means well. I am so proud to call him my Pastor, My Father in the Ministry, My Brother and My Friend.

I love you Pastor Jermal Boddie, Sr. I thank God for you and everything you have done for me! I am forever grateful. Your Daughter in the Ministry,   Minister Amy

3

HE CALLS ME TEE TEE

When I met him, it was like meeting someone I had known a long time. He wasn't a stranger, very polite, very friendly. He made everyone feel special. He calls me TeeTee, and sometimes Minister Cousins, but mostly TeeTee, which is fine. We are all like family at Grace. I really like Pastor Boddie, he keeps you laughing and includes everyone. I pray much for him and his family. He is truly a special man.
Love TeeTee, Minister Clea Cousins.

4
====

HE IS TOUGH ON US MINISTERS

I met Pastor Jermal Boddie some years ago, he didn't talk much then. He seemed to be a quiet person at that time. Whenever he saw me, he would always invite me over to fellowship with his church 'Grace Baptist Church ' in Okolona, MS.

I never went, until I met this young lady by the name of Amy Lamesia Deanes. I went to her first initial sermon and that's were it all begin.

He allowed me to preach at his church and I immediately became a part of his church family.

He always encouraged me to release the gift, in which God has placed in me. He knew that God had a special gift on the inside of me and I needed to let it out. He was tough on all of us minister and he only wanted the best for us.

He would fuss and call us out, because he didn't want us lacking in any area of our life.

He taught us to lead and to reach people on every level.

He is a great Pastor and a good listening ear, when we needed to talk. I Thank God for his leadership and only want the best that God has for him.

He has a big vision for Grace Baptist Church and he's trusting God for bigger and better things to transform in the body of Christ.

He preaches with fire and doesn't mind stepping on your toes. All you can do is say 'ouch!"

I Thank God for his leadership and all the encouraging words that he has spoken in my life!

God Bless You, Pastor Jermal Boddie Sr!
Evangelist Linda Townsend

5

THE DAY I MET AN ANGEL

    Back in 2005 when I met this fellow I felt like I had just met an angel. After that day my life was never the same. He became my friend, my brother and my Pastor. His goal was to lead people to Jesus and once he laid hands on me there was no turning back. He's a friend that laugh , cry and pray with you and for you. He's a brother that you can be real with and he will get on your level to help you rise to his. He's a WONDERFUL PASTOR that brings out the best in you and make Everyone feel like Somebody. He helps people to see their worth in life. He will help anybody anywhere. He's a man with actions to back up his words.

He's always striving to make the community and everything and everyone around him better.

Jackie Allen

6

YOU TOOK THE LITTLE GOD GAVE YOU

Oct. 2016...In spite of the circumstances you were a man with desire and determination on the inside of you to keep doing what you loved doing. You had a plan from day one that nothing and no one could stop, especially the enemy.

I remember ALL the phone calls and conversations that started " Hey what you think about this" I knew it was something about GRACE, and if you had already thought about it you were going to do it..Although there were a few times when I said "NO" (LOL). I listened to you speak things into existence (for your first love Grace)and I also watched you work day and night to make it happen- "Faith without works is dead"

I remember there were days of uncertainty or when you felt like giving up and I had to put YOUR OWN WORDS ON YOU PREACHER!!

You wouldn't let that drive and determination to keep working for God go and the enemy lost again..The church was FAR from what you envisioned but you showed Patience, Determination and Perseverance and it has really paid off.. You took the "LITTLE" God gave you and made it "MUCH". Much as in "where everybody is somebody " Much praise and worship. Much love is shown through your teaching of giving back to God and each other.

I know God is pleased with what you have done with what He gave you. I'm thankful for all that I have learned and how I have grown spiritually through your teaching. I know that there has been a renewing of my mind and my faith is stronger than ever because of your teaching and preaching. I pray for your health and strength to keep doing what God wants you to do. I'm thankful for all the happy memories we have shared on this life changing journey at Grace.

        May God Bless and Keep you..I love you.

        Tangi Donaldson

7
===

V.I.P. STATUS

Rev Boddie!!!
Is a friend first and foremost, we've gone through some struggles together, and drew strength from each other. It seemed like when things were bad for him I was strong.And at some of my lowest mo-

ments, he was always there to encourage me. He means a lot to me and my family.

All the times he made me laugh, I can't count them, but I'll always remember the trip to Jackson to our state championship game. We were in a SUV and a car, he parked us in the VIP section and went through the side door and nobody paid a dime to get in.

Rev Boddie is truly a rare breed! A community pastor, leader and friend to all that will let him be. We don't find that in people too much nowadays .
Thank you for being a friend.
William Bailey, Sr.

8

WHAT GOES ON IN BILOXI STAYS IN BILOXI

    I am so grateful to have a caring pastor a giving pastor a pastor that is concerned about people and the community. Pastor Boddie is concerned about the young people and there life. Pastor Boddie is a pastor who enjoy life and tell his members to enjoy life love God put God first then everything thing else will work out for your good. Remembering our church trip to Biloxi how we all had lots of laughter just enjoying each other and life. We had a joke everything done in Biloxi stay in Biloxi ????. We had a blast just to let you know you can be a Christian and have good clean fun. If you want to have a day full of laughter just go on a trip with pastor Boddie. He will make you welcome and loved know one is left out. Pastor I love you my family loves you and appreciate you more than you will ever know. Keep fighting, keep pressing, keep believing, and continue to hold on to God Unchanging Hand. When you are at your lowest point remember God sees, He knows, and He cares, He's holding you in His hand. It's sooo awesome to have a pastor with a giving heart and has faith in God. He listens to the Lord and he stands on God's word. It's also good to have a pastor with a vision he's a visionary. The Bible says Without a vision the people perish. Stay connected with God. Don't loose hope. Love you pastor. God is in control!!!!

Naomi Bailey, Mama Bailey

9

HE WHIPPED ME LIKE HE WAS MY DADDY

So one of my most memorable (not necessarily fond, but memorable) moments with Elliott was when I was about 8 years old. I was staying the weekend with his mother, Jean, and for some reason Elliott just did not want to be bothered, so he closed himself off in his room. He was usually so much fun, but I can only assume the devil got into him that particular day. Not being deterred by his stank attitude, I knocked on his door repeatedly, and he kept telling me I better not come in. Finally, I just went in, and he grabbed a belt and whipped me like he was my daddy. Elliott is only about 10 years older than me, so I was shocked he thought he could get away with that. I got myself together and went back up front to tell Jean what Elliott had done because I was sure she would light into him. As Jean sat at the table, smoking her cigarette, she listened to me and responded, "didn't he tell you not to take your butt in there?" I learned to respect Elliott's boundaries that day, and we've been good ever since!

After I got a little older, one of my favorite things to do with Elliott was ride because he always had a nice vehicle. Elliott would drive fast, have music blasting, and everybody would be looking. During those rides, Elliott would take me wherever I wanted to go, and he always gave me little nuggets of "street sense" along the way. All in all, I really appreciate how generous Elliott was with his time, and over the course of my 43 years, he has been like a brother to me. I love him dearly.
-Nikki

10

HE SAW SOMETHING IN ME

Father God I come now thanking you for Pastor Boddie, Father God asking that you will continuously protect him, cover him, lead and guide him. Lord I thank you for the day that I crossed paths with him, he saw something in me that needed grooming, he believed in me when I really didn't believe in myself. Lord I am forever grateful for that. Strengthen his heart and mind daily, direct him Lord and show him Your way. Lead and guide him Lord in the path of righteousness for Your Name sake. Lord when he doesn't know which way, give him direction. Lord when he doesn't know what to say put words in his mouth. Lord when his thoughts are clouded, give him Your thoughts. Lord as he comes to a new chapter in his life, give him more spiritual insight and a stronger discernment to know who to trust in this season. Father God we ask that you will give him an unlimited supply of finances to do work for Your kingdom. Lord I thank You now for Your man of God and as You continue to lead him let him continue to lead Your people. In Jesus Name. Amen

Kay

11

HE PULLED SOMETHING OUT OF ME

Where do I began My Pastor, Friend and Brother. I have known Pastor B(PB) for over 15 years. I have had the privilege of being under his leadership in two "different " places. The atmosphere were also totally opposite of each other. Today, i can honestly say I have I grown under His current leadership. He has pulled things out of me that we suppressed…However being able to understand the Man of God and Him serving in His purpose has had an awesome impact on my life. The love and support that PB shows and gives when needed the most is just wonderful. Thank you PB for all that you do it does not go unnoticed….

Sonya

12

HE KNOWS HOW TO REEL IT IN...

Pastor Boddie is more like a friend than a pastor. We talked most days at some point. Whenever there's something going on involving church business he sometimes call me and ask me " Dea, what you think" usually we' re on the same page. Whenever you go on trip with him, you are sure to have a great time filled with fun and laughter. The wisdom he has is far beyond his years both naturally and spiritually. He love serving others and seeing them reach their full potential.He knows how to have fun and not take life too seriously but he also knows how to reel it in and deal with the serious issues of life. I am honored to serve under him and call him my Pastor.
       Deacon Walker

13

HE NEVER CLOSED THE DOORS DURING THE PANDEMIC

    I appreciate pastor Boddie for never closing the doors in the midst of the pandemic. It was an honor to be able to still do the live streams while a lot of pastors had closed the doors. Boddie is a very true man of God and I am truly glad to call him my pastor.

By preaching the Word of the Lord, you allow our faith community to experience the joy of God's presence.

Thank you for your work as a pastor and thank you for being the glue that brings this community together!

DESTINI

14

HE CALLS ME HIS HONORARY MEMBER

When I first met Pastor Boddie it was as if we had known each other for years. I love that he NEVER meets a stranger, he acts as if you're best friends from day one. I also love his love for people and his desire to see everyone make it. I call him my honorary Pastor and he calls me his honorary member because whenever I'm at Grace he treats me as if I'm part of the flock. I have so much respect for him and his love for God. He is definitely a very special person.
Jessie Mae

15

YOU NEVER JUDGED HIM

    Thank you for being there for my brother at a time in his life that he had no where else to go. You let him come live with you, helped him get a job, gave him an apartment and called him out on his BS. You never judged him but held him accountable for his actions. Words could never express my gratitude for all that you did for him. You were 1st cousins but grew up as brothers. You understood him because you had been through some of the same things so he couldn't fool you.

You saw the best in him and got to see him turn his life around.

I'm thankful for the call that's on your life. Continue doing what God's says and watch Him show out on your behalf!

Love you, Sharon

16

YOU DIDN'T HESISTATE

Thank you, Bishop, for being a part of one of the most important days of Inaya's (Wild Sally) life. When I asked you to baptize her you didn't hesitate and said you'd be honored to do it. At a time when churches make things like a business, you made her baptism special.

I know your parents, grandma and the rest of the family in heaven are looking down on you and are so very proud of the Man of God that you are. We speak blessings upon blessings over you always!

Love,
Sharon (Sister Cousin) & Inaya (Wild Sally aka Cousin/Niece)

17

HE REACHES OUT TO ME FIRST

Pastor Boddie is a real pastor and a real person. He's honest and cuts no corners. He's inspired me in many ways in just the few years I've been knowing him. He's become more than just a pastor to me, but also family. Whenever I'm low, (and it's almost like he knows every time), because I don't have to reach out to him, instead he reaches out to me first. I thank God for him and wouldn't change him for the world! Love you Big Brother Pastor!!

Angelica

18

HE WILL LAUGH WHEN YOU LAUGH AND CRY WHEN YOU CRY

Pastor Jermal Boddie is a lively, authentic, and energetic preacher! Not only is he skilled at bringing the Word of God but he's also a friend and a brother in Christ. He finds joy in the Word and embraces the worship experience. He has a generous spirit and loves helping in the community.
While he cherishes his family, what's most exciting and admirable about Pastor Boddie is the way he delivers the word of God in a way that even a child can understand. He knows how to make connections with young people and has the ability to get people excited about being saved and living right.
To know him personally, as a friend, know that he will support your endeavors. Whether you have a personal goal or business venture, he will give good sound advice, encouragement, and especially lift you in prayer. Furthermore, as a brother in Christ, he will laugh when you laugh and cry when you cry. If you feel joy, he feels joy; if you feel pain, he feels pain; if you

want to get your praise on, he will dance, jump, and shout in the name of Jesus alongside you. If you need someone to talk to, he's always willing to listen. When you just want to have a good time, he's the life of the party! He loves to have a good time!

In short, a tribute to Pastor Boddie to celebrate the ministry and encouragement that we all know and love him for:
   There is only One who sticks closer than a brother,
        but you, my friend, are clearly another
who shows yourself friendly and shows yourself kind;
     Sharer of truth and speaking your mind...
As the Good Shepherd leads so you continue to guide
  with the Holy Spirit within and right by your side.
       I'm grateful for your attentive ear
    and thankful that you are always here.
    When in pain or sorrow you offer prayer
  and especially in joy you're always there.
       To know you is to love you more
  And I truly am grateful for all your support.
   Your strength never wavers nor does it bend;
  Thank you, dear brother, for being my friend!
          -Autumn Bankhead

19

I KNEW THAT HE WAS DIFFERENT

I met pastor Boddie at Midway Baptist church. He was preaching a revival there, he had a sense of humor when he preached he was a good teacher but I knew that he was different from the others their he was jumping into the Apostolic some. A couple years later I see him again at Pontotoc jail he was doing a movement there of teaching while me and a lady was teaching at the jail. I never knew that I would grow closer to Grace Baptist and feel so welcome by him and Grace Baptist. He is a lover of teaching, he is transparent and that's what we need. He has helped me personally by encouraging me to keep going in God's word. He has helped many women in general to feel appreciated and needed in the kingdom to let God use Us. I do know there is a prophetic mantle on him stronger than just prophecy, but to go deeper in God. He has been hurt, rejected, abused, neglected, back-stabbed, and has made personal mistakes along the way yet Pastor Boddie strives to repent, and start all over again trying to REACH God's people. Pastor Boddie I pray you get closer to God go deeper with him and soar like an eagle of God and roar like the lion of Judah

Evangelist Shalaura McKinney

20

HE TELLS IT LIKE IT IS

THE ROGERS FAMILY LOVE YOU

Rev is more than a Pastor to my family & I. He has become family to the Rogers. He is constantly pouring into us. Sometimes the thing he says doesn't feel good to the ears BUT it's exactly what we need to hear. He is a tell it like it is person. That's what I love most about a him. I love what God is doing in his life & I can't wait to see the rainbows that comes from the storms that he has endured.

YOCHIA

I would like to say that he is an inspiration to me and my family. We consider him a part of our family. We love you

DIANNE

Russell & Rick

21

HE'S BEEN THROUGH A STORM LIKE US

Boddie is a Grand Champ! I love the way he talk. He is a great guy to me! We both been through storms.

Rick aka Boosie

Denise and Mrs. Florida

22

I KNOW HOW HARD YOU'VE BEEN WORKING

I want to encourage you that your labor is not in vain. I know how hard you have been working and want to remind you that Jesus is worth it all!
Congratulation. and keep spreading the good news of the gospel!
love Denise Buchanan and Mama Florida

23

A POEM FOR PASTOR BODDIE

A Poem for Pastor Boddie
Well where do I start
He's the dude with the million dollar smile,
and the world biggest heart.

He always got a word and He'll
tell you to your face.
And before the conversation ends,
He'll invite you to Grace.
He has a personality like no one I ever seen
And if you didn't know him well
You would think he's really mean.

And what I like about him
He'll meet you where you are.
You are never to big, never to small
And it doesn't matter how far.

He opens his doors to everyone
man, woman, boy and girl.
He can pull the best of the best
from all over the world.

His mind is always open, to big
and better things.
When He get to Heaven, God may have to clip his wings.

He proclaims the word of God,
His teachings is very clear.
You may be at the wrong place
If you want teaching that tickles the ear.

Well I really love Pastor Boddie
And he really loves His church.
Cause He is always having something
No matter who says it's to much!

He accepts God preacher men,
women and children, when they answer God's Call.

He's not one to discriminate
He knows God loves us all.

Pastor Boddie is really cool,
and stay on top of his game.
If His name wasn't Pastor Boddie,
Sega Genesis and Nintendo would be his middle name

Well In my closing I just want to say
He love my favorite dish.
That's dig some baits, grab a pole and go down to the pool and fish.
Happy Anniversary Pastor Boddie!
Frances

24

WE ARE BLESSED TO HAVE YOU

Hey Dad,
If we were to write the reasons that we are grateful for you on a little piece of paper, they would fill up an entire room.
You are amazing and hardworking .
We are blessed to have you in our life.
Thank you for everything that you are .
Love,
LaKourtney, Jamiya, Antwaun, Jermal, and Javarrian.

25

EMARIE

My fondest memory of my dad is when Erynn and I went to eat at Hunan in Amory with him. After placing our order, they stuck a pot with a broom stick on it outside the drive-thru window to collect our money. My dad said, "What is this?" in his best impression of a Chinese voice.

Love Emarie

26
═══════

MY DAD TAUGHT ME NOTHING IS IMPOSSIBLE

My dad has taught me that nothing is impossible. He always encourages me to do my best at whatever I'm doing. My dad has taught me how to be strong minded and kind. And for that, I am thankful.
Love Erynn

27

I LEARN FROM HIM...

My favorite thing about my dad is that he always has my back. We travel everywhere together and I learn from him while we travel. My dad is smart and funny. My dad will help anybody. It doesn't matter what they need. He will try to help.

Love Emerson

28

MY DAD HAS DONE MANY THINGS FOR ME

There are many things my dad has done for me. The one that comes to mind at the moment is him getting a car for me even though I'm not ready to drive it. And for that, I am grateful.   Love EJ

29

IT'S SOMETHING ABOUT YOU THAT MAKES IT HARD TO SAY NO

Uncle Elliott, I feel a special closeness to you. I guess it's because through the years, you've been there..cheering me on, encouraging me, listening to my troubles, and giving me a laugh along the way. It's something about you that makes it hard to say no to your requests. Lol! I'm sure that your sisters will agree. It's nothing for you to call randomly with encouragement and words of advice and it seems like it's always when I need it most. You have always been the fun uncle-so full of life. You give freely to others, without conditions, never looking for anything in return. God has truly blessed and kept you and for that I am so grateful. I thank God that he has afforded me this chance to tell you how much I love you and how much you mean to me while you can yet hear and see the love. You are truly one of a kind and I love you dearly, Unc! Love Krystal

Hey there Pastor! I want to let you know that I'm going to step in and take care of your church if something happens to you. I love you and can't wait for us to travel to churches together when I get older.
Love you! Your nephew, Treyson

30

BIG BROTHER, LITTLE BROTHER

As I reflect over last fifty plus years, it has been a fascinating journey with this man of God as a younger sibling. Growing up has been laugh after laugh and some tears in between as well. Since his early days,

Jermal has always been a handful. There are just to many to reflect on but the most important one is the day he answered his call to the ministry. It was a time of turmoil, him fighting the Devil and standing steadfast on the Word of God, but with the help of The Lord, he's won battle after battle after battle. Not to say he hasn't lost a few, but most definitely more victories than losses. Simply put, I do believe he is a man of God. A wise woman once said that after the Devil has run out of things for you to do then The Lord would handle it from there. Her prophecy was given when he was just a lad and at fifty-two years of age, it is coming into fruition. The bond between my brother and I is just like marriage "till death do us part." I truly love you Reverend Jermal Boddie, continue to stand tall and most importantly, keep the faith.?

Others pictures by Claud Boddie, Jr.

31

YOU MADE SURE YOU SHARED WITH ME

You are definitely a family oriented person and I love that about you. You have had our backs from Day One! You and I have been rocking and rolling for a long time and the memories I have are etched in my mind forever. In particular when you preached your first sermon, I was overjoyed that God spared your life for such a time as this (being called into ministry). That night, you said that the devil thought he had you down for the count, 1, 2, 3.... BUT, your foot was on the rope! Thank you Lord!

When you hit a low point in life and I couldn't help you, I cried, I prayed, I cried some more, and then I let you go to God. It wasn't easy for me to let go; however, you were wrestling with the spiritual wickedness of the world. Thank God I had enough sense to realize I had to turn you over to Jesus....and....let him work it out. During this time I admit that you missed out on a lot, Fortunately, God knows that you have tried and are trying to make up for lost time.

I thank God that mom and dad got the opportunity to witness this change. Happy Anniversary my brother. May you enjoy this year and many years to come.

    Unapologetically, I love you.
      Kim

32

YOU ARE PROBABLY WONDERING WHY EVERYONE CALLS HIM JERMAL

As this little soul began to thrive in his mothers womb, we were trying to decide what shall we name him. My cousin Gail won by naming him Elliott after the actor on Mod Squad.The very first time I laid eyes on Elliot Jermal Boddie was such an amazement to me because I was only six years old.From that day forward I always considered him as my baby! I became his second mother and most of all his protector.

Going to church all of his life, I can remember at his tender age of three, Elliott would go into the church and head straight to the pulpit. Deacon Clifton "Duck"Coleman would say ,boy one day you are going to be a preacher! I thank God,that was spoken into his spirit at an early age. Elliott was not your aver-

age kid. He loved to play in the ditch behind our house And catch octopuses as he would call them although they were actually crawdads that he was catching. Lol. He loved to fish, hunt, play jokes, and loved his pet dog Lady.

So, you are probably wondering why everyone calls him Jermal. Well, when mom signed him up for

Head Start, his birth certificate came back and read Jermal Boddie. Elliott had been left off of his birth certificate.So he had to start going by the name of Jermal. At the day of his Head Start graduation, my Momma took so many pictures.....my grandmother said Jean, why are you taking so many pictures? Mom replied, This joker may not have another graduation in his life! So, I am going to take all the pictures I can right now.

Beginning elementary school was a real big hassle. He wanted to go back to Head Start.He gave poor Kim the blues! He would walk to the corner stop and sit down and tell Kim I am not going to school .She had to pull him to school. Kim told mom and she gave his but a good whipping and from that day forward, he probably had some reservations but, he went to school with no problem. Jermal was such a character in school until all teachers,students, just everyone knew Jermal. As he matriculated onto middle school he became an avid swimmer on the swim team. He could swim like a fish. That meant the world to him. Upon completion of middle school he attended East Side High school and became a Trojan die-hard.As I stated, he was not your typical kid. He would often be caught daydreaming.When asked about this problem all he was thinking about how he could go fishing, hunting , or what type of mischievous acts he could do with Lee Dale Collins, Darryl and Varrian Hall . One morning,Daddy received a phone call from the assistant principal stating that Jermal had been cutting up sideways in class. The assistant principal said , Mr.Boddie we are going to have going to send him home. Daddy said, what are you sending him home for, ain't nothing I can do with him at home. Whip his _ _ _ and send him to class! During his senior year of high school, Jermal was so close to graduation. The counselor, Mrs. Jordan, called and stated that he wasn't going to graduate because he was failing a class. Kim and I immediately headed to the school and big the teacher, What can he do to pass your class. He said, you know, Jermal just come in class, put his head down and go to sleep. He doesn't turn in his homework and sometimes he plays hooky.He will have to make an A on his final exam to pass this class.So that weekend, Jermal could not do anything but study! He could only come out of his room to use the restroom , eat, and go to church on Sunday. I tell you what , my Mom , a strong prayer Warrior , prayed a powerful prayer at the alter !!! The next day Jermal took that test and smoked it with an A !!! Mama said ,you could have been doing that all the time.We were so grateful and thankful to God because we knew he had to go ahead and join the Navy!

As we all know life doesn't always go as we planned.Sometimes there are twists and turns along the path. Instead of going on the right path,sometimes we may take a left .Jermal certainly had his battles but, he had to refer back to his foundation.At one point in his life , he said , he was at the bottom and all he could do was look up. I thank God for his grace and mercy, I thank God for blessing our family with some powerful prayer warriors, and a firm foundation from our parents and grandparents!I also thank God for blessing Jermal to speak God's words for God's vision. He teaches God's words because he wants mankind to reap the benefits of God's kingdom .I admire the fact,how he ministers to the young and the old.I love the way, Pastor Boddie has a love for our family and how he embraces his church family, all of his brothers and sisters in Christ. Most of all, I love the fact, He loves the Lord!

Sooo...Baby brother on this day, I salute you and I love you always and forever!

      Tracey Sanders

HE IS VERY SUPPORTIVE TO HIS FAMILY AND FRIENDS

My Cousin Jamal: Jamal loves the Lord, his church, children and his family. He is very supportive to his family and friends. Jamal is doing what the Lord has called on him to do; preach the word. He realizes that if the Lord calls you, he will also prepare you. I am very proud to tell everyone that he is my family. I have

watched how he lovingly teaches and guides his children in a fatherly manner. He's a good Dad!
Congratulations Rev. Boddie on your Third Anniversary!
Regenia Haley

33
===

CLASS OF 87

34

THERE IS NO WAY ONE MAD DID ALL OF THAT

My friend and brother from another mother, we met in the first grade and grew up on the same block. His magnetic and humorous personality instantly made him the center of attention in and out of school. He certainly was the class clown and would do ANYTHING for a laugh. I've sat in the company of others who grew up with him and we would tell Jermal Boddie stories for hours and laugh until we hurt. Those of us who joined the military or moved away, would share our stories with our new friends and they would listen in disbelief. They would often respond by saying, "There is no way one man did all of that!" We literally grew up as if we were real brothers and both of our families are connected at the hip. I've seen his regression and lows as well as his ascension to the man he has become. No one could have predicted that he would one day be leading others from the pulpit. God saw fit to reach down and save my brother from himself and put him on a path in which he was able to use his personality and gifts to lead others to HIM. I am certainly proud of Mr. Boddie and I look forward to what God has planned for him next!

On a final note, I can not conclude without sharing at least one Jermal Boddie story that we've laughed about for years. He and my cousin would steal Jermal's mom car at night and go joyriding while she was asleep. They would do this by putting the car in neutral, pushing it from the the carport, and then down the street before cranking it. Jermal's father, Mr. Boddie, was a police officer. This particular night while Jermal and my cousin were pushing the car down the street, Officer Boddie was on duty and decided to drive by his house. Jermal spotted his dad in the patrol car coming down the street and vanished without warning or saying anything to my cousin who was busy still pushing the car. As you would imagine, when Mr. Boddie saw that his family car was being pushed down the street by some unsuspecting car thief, he rushed out of his car, drew his weapon and said,

"FREEZE!!" My cousin was so scared and shocked, all he could say was, "Don't Shoot Mr. Boddie, It's Me!!" Suddenly, Jermal jumps from out of nowhere yelling, "WE GOT EM DADDY, WE GOT EM!"

35

HE PREACHED ON A LEVEL ALL GROUPS AND AGES COULD UNDERSTAND

When I first met Rev. Jermal Boddie, I was a member of Mt. Calvary Holiness Outreach church under the leadership of Rev. Hudson L. Williams. I remember this young man walking in the church strutting up the aisle cool as a cucumber. I watched him as he took a seat in the pulpit and my thoughts were, "Oh he's a preacher."
I shrugged it off thinking he must be a friend of the Pastor Williams.
That same Sunday our church was going out to eat after service. I wasn't going because my funds was low but I didn't tell anyone. Only God and I knew.
Rev. Boddie was at the podium introducing himself to the congregation. I was again thinking to myself, "I don't know any Boddies " All of a sudden I heard him say, "I'm going to pay for her meal today." That "her" was me! He was looking straight at me and I was like, How did he know?" I quickly realized that God had touched his heart to bless me. I was so amazed at how a total stranger could come in and bless another total stranger as if it was a natural act but really it was a spiritual act of kindness that to this day, I have never forgotten.
My first time hearing him preach almost blew my mind. He preached on a level that all groups and ages could relate to. His preaching style was different. He has a drawing spirit that some envy but can't duplicate. Over the years he and have remained friends. To see what God is doing in his life right now is totally awesome. I thank God for putting His anointed vessel in my life.

Minister Melissa
Poem
And God called Boddie with a still small voice
"Boddie Boddie"
But Boddie didn't answer right away
He was still caught up in the world
And like a little child, he still wanted to play

God called Boddie once again
And this time He was very firm
Boddie knew that all too familiar voice
Right then and there he made his choice
There were somethings he had to leave behind
There were somethings he had to give up
God never told him it would be easy
He remembered that when times got tough
But he held on to prayer and fath
Amid the tempestuous storms and pain
Trusting and believing in God
That his situation would somehow change
Like King David he is a warrior
Like old man Job he is patient
Like Nehemiah he is a focused builder
A man that is determined to make it
He has battle scars we don't see
He has a heart we all can feel
He has a deaf ear to all nay sayers
A man striving to just keep it real
So when you see this man of God
Show some kindness and due respect
Because just like you and i
God is not through with him yet!!

36

GREATER GRACE

To my friend, Pastor Boddie,
Congrats!!
May God continue to bless you keep you is my prayer.
May God constantly and continually bless your work
and worship at Greater Grace!
Pastor Alphonzo Bowen

37

HE JUST KEPT SAYING WATCH GOD

I can't really find the words to express how I feel about this brother without crying. Jermal Boddie is just more than a friend or just a colleague but he is my true Brother. I have had moments in my life and ministry when so many cut out of the good old boy system. He told me that God is much bigger than
 any system in place. He told me that God is shifting things for me to do more than I could ever imagine. He always has been a great encouragement to me.
 He just kept saying watch God work.

I've known Boddie for over 20 years and he has always been the same kind of guy. Straight forward and to the point. If it's anything that he doesn't like you would know it. He truly takes brotherhood to the heart.

I can't say that about many but this guy here is truly one of a kind. He has been there for me when so many times when others have counted me out and Dead.

                    Dr. Benjamin Curry

38

HE'S NOT A FRIEND OF MINE, BUT MY BIG BROTHER

Words cannot actually express how I feel about my brother Boddie. We've been there for each other's good times, bad times, happy times & sad times. But, through it all, we made it and we are still here.
He's not a friend of mine but he's a big brother. I will never forget the bond we share .
Whatever I have he's most definitely welcome to share it or have it. Thanks for always supporting me in whatever I do !

Pastor Orlando Franklin

39

YOU HAVE ALWAYS BEEN A TRUE BROTHER

I just want to say congratulations to my brother my friend my call labor in the ministry I remember when we made over 20/30 years ago in Cleveland Mississippi when you were working at and run in your family on dry cleaner On the low in Cleveland you have always been a true brother you have always been a true friend and when God made Jermal Boddie he only made one and I want to tell you I appreciate you for your loyalty I appreciate you for your friendship and a definite appreciate you for your brotherhood I pray that God continue to bless you may God continue to bless your ministry and I pray that God continue to give you the desires of your heart and one thing you can rest of sure you have a brother and me and like you say 4 life. Pastor Moshiu T. Knox

40

HIS YES IS A YES

One of the consistent qualities of Jermal BODDIE is that he's TRUE to his Family, Church & Friends. His YES is a YES & he honors Loyalty.

We met well over 20+ years ago & have continued to strengthen our True Brotherhood. He has a LOVE for Grace Baptist & the people of Okolona. God bless you my brother on your anniversary.

    Pastor Kenneth Turner, St. James Bible Fellowship in St. Louis, Mo.

Thank you Woman Of God for this great tribute. God bless!

41

FRIENDS TIL THE END

"THE GROUND IS NO PLACE FOR A CHAMPION,
GET UP BODDIE!"

Even though Bishop Sparks is no longer here, I know how much he cared for you, so I couldn't leave him out. I'm sure he would have shared many things. But you have your memories. Cherish those.

Rest On Bishop Sparks

    As you can see, I'm not the only Author. The Lord laid it on my heart to do this for such a great person and to let other people that loved and wanted to celebrate him, help celebrate him as well. Just recently, I taught about Moses and his rod, "Use What's In Your Hand" and that stuck with me. I have a laptop and a publishing company, use it!

    Thank you to every person that participated, you made your place in the book! And I know Pastor is overjoyed. Just reading what you all wrote made me happy, and it was about him. He's a Great Ministry Father to me, brother and a friend when I need one. He always takes me to the Word when I'm upset and want to move in the flesh. I'm not always happy about that, but I know it's right.

    Pastor Boddie as you can see, you are appreciated.

www.ingramcontent.com/pod-product-compliance
Lightning Source LLC
Chambersburg PA
CBHW040202100526
44592CB00001B/7